Rookie
STAR™
Extraordinary
Animals

Cool Camouflage

Lisa M. Herrington

Content Consultant
Curatorial Team
Columbus Zoo and Aquarium, Columbus, Ohio

Reading Consultant
Jeanne M. Clidas, Ph.D.
Reading Specialist

Children's Press®
An Imprint of Scholastic Inc.

Library of Congress Cataloging-in-Publication Data
Names: Herrington, Lisa M., author.
Title: Cool camouflage: Giraffes! Tigers! Seals!/by Lisa M. Herrington.
Description: New York, NY: Children's Press, an imprint of Scholastic Inc., 2018. |
Series: Rookie STAR. Extraordinary animals
Identifiers: LCCN 2017025795 | ISBN 9780531230909 (library binding) |
ISBN 9780531233795 (pbk.)
Subjects: LCSH: Animals—Color—Juvenile literature. | Camouflage (Biology)—Juvenile literature. |
Protective coloration (Biology)—Juvenile literature.
Classification: LCC QL767 .H48 2018 | DDC 591.47/2—dc23
LC record available at https://lccn.loc.gov/2017025795

Produced by Spooky Cheetah Press
Art direction: Keith Plechaty for kwpCreative
Creative direction: Judith E. Christ for Scholastic
Art direction: Brenda Jackson for Scholastic

Published in 2019 by Children's Press, an imprint of Scholastic Inc.

Printed in Johor Bahru, Malaysia 108

SCHOLASTIC, CHILDREN'S PRESS, ROOKIE STAR™, and associated logos are trademarks and/or
registered trademarks of Scholastic Inc.

2 3 4 5 6 7 8 9 10 R 28 27 26 25 24 23 22 21 20 19

Scholastic Inc., 557 Broadway, New York, NY 10012.

Photographs ©: cover: Werner Bollmann/age fotostock; 1: karinegenest/iStockphoto; 2: Ryan M.
Bolton/Shutterstock; 3: carolthacker/iStockphoto; 4-5: Claus Meyer/Minden Pictures/Superstock,
Inc.; 6-7: Ingo Arndt/NPL/Minden Pictures; 8-9: FLPA/Malcolm Schuyl /age fotostock; 9 inset:
Angelika/iStockphoto; 10 inset: blickwinkel/Alamy Images; 10-11: NHPA/Superstock, Inc.; 12
inset: Werner Bollmann/age fotostock; 12-13: Troels Jacobsen/Arcticphoto/NPL/Minden Pictures;
13 inset: Matthias Breiter/Minden Pictures; 14-15: Premaphotos/NPL/Minden Pictures; 15 inset:
imageBROKER/Alamy Images; 16-17: Fred Bavendam/Minden Pictures; 17 inset: Ethan Daniels/
WaterFrame/age fotostock; 18 inset: atosf/iStockphoto; 18-19: Patricio Robles Gil/Sierra Madre/
Minden Pictures; 20-21: Thomas Marentant/Pantheon/Superstock, Inc.; 21 inset: Unno Kazuo/
Nature Production/Minden Pictures; 22 inset: Sandesh Kadur/NPL/Minden Pictures; 22-23:
Edwin Giesbers/NPL/Minden Pictures; 24-25: agf photo/Superstock, Inc.; 25 inset: Ariadne
Van Zandbergen/Getty Images; 26 inset: Michael-Tatman/iStockphoto; 26-27: McPHOTO/age
fotostock; 28 top: Konrad Wothe/Minden Pictures; 28 inset: David & Micha Sheldon/Thinkstock;
28-29 ribbons: _human/iStockphoto; 29 top: Ron and Valerie Tay/age fotostock; 29 inset:
Divelvanov/iStockphoto; 30 top: FLPA/Superstock, Inc.; 30 bottom left: Mitsuhiko Imamori/
Nature Production/Minden Pictures; 30 bottom right: Pascal Kobeh/NPL/Minden Pictures; 30 top
right: Christian Ziegler/Minden Pictures; 31 center top: atosf/iStockphoto; 31 bottom: Angelika/
iStockphoto; 31 center bottom: agf photo/Superstock, Inc.; 31 top: Claus Meyer/Minden Pictures/
Superstock, Inc.; 32: Pete Oxford/age fotostock.

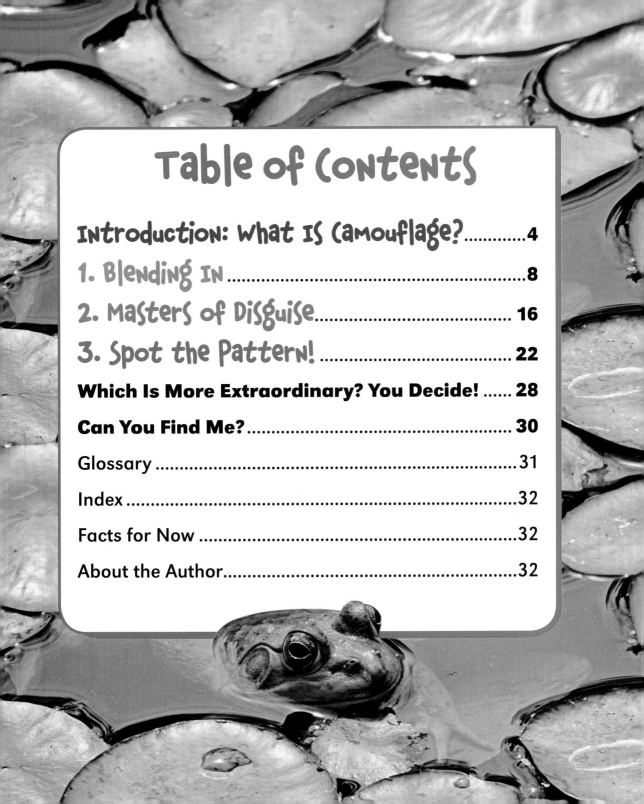

Table of Contents

What Is Camouflage?

Can you find the frog? This little leaper is tricky to spot. The ability of an animal to blend in with its surroundings is called **camouflage**. This green frog hides among the leaves. Other animals cannot see it.

This Brazilian tree frog is hiding in the leaves of a water plant.

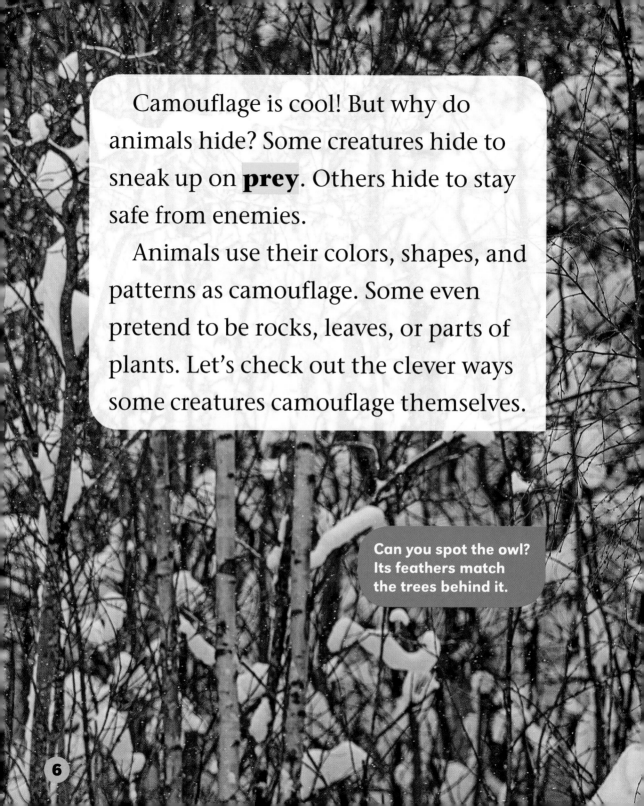

Camouflage is cool! But why do animals hide? Some creatures hide to sneak up on **prey**. Others hide to stay safe from enemies.

Animals use their colors, shapes, and patterns as camouflage. Some even pretend to be rocks, leaves, or parts of plants. Let's check out the clever ways some creatures camouflage themselves.

Can you spot the owl? Its feathers match the trees behind it.

Chapter 1

Blending In

Many **predators** use their color as camouflage. This lioness's golden-brown fur blends in with the tall, dry grasses of Africa's plains. This background matching is one form of camouflage. But predators are not the only animals that try to blend in. Their prey do, too. Even lion cubs need to stay hidden. They are too small to protect themselves from other animals.

A lioness uses camouflage to sneak up on prey.

Impala are among the lion's favorite prey. They hide behind the tall grasses to stay safe. An impala's tan color helps it blend right in.

Snakes use camouflage to find food and stay safe. How they look depends on where they live. Sidewinders wear a desert disguise. Their brown skin matches the sand. This helps them catch lizards and mice. Small horns over their eyes keep out sand.

Some snakes live in trees. This green vine snake winds itself through the leafy branches. It is almost invisible to prey!

A sidewinder buries most of its body in the sand.

Some animals have amazing skills! They camouflage themselves by actually changing color. In winter, an Arctic fox's white fur helps it hide in the snow. But surprise! In summer, its coat turns brown or gray. Then the fox blends in with the rocks.

This baby harp seal was born with fluffy white fur. The fur helps the seal hide from fierce polar bears. As seals grow, they lose their white coats. Adult seals may be a yellowish or gray color. They spend more time in the water, where a white coat would not help!

In winter, the fox covers its black nose with its tail to disappear in the snow.

The fox's summer coat provides better camouflage when the snow is gone.

13

Bees and butterflies, beware! This goldenrod crab spider is a deadly hunter. It doesn't spin a web, though. Instead, it hides among a flower's yellow petals. It waits for a bee to get close. Then it grabs the insect with its legs and bites with its fangs. On a white flower, the spider slowly changes its color to match.

Why do chameleons change colors? Many people think they do it as camouflage to match their surroundings. But that is not true. These lizards actually change colors to show their mood. This lets other chameleons know when they are scared or excited.

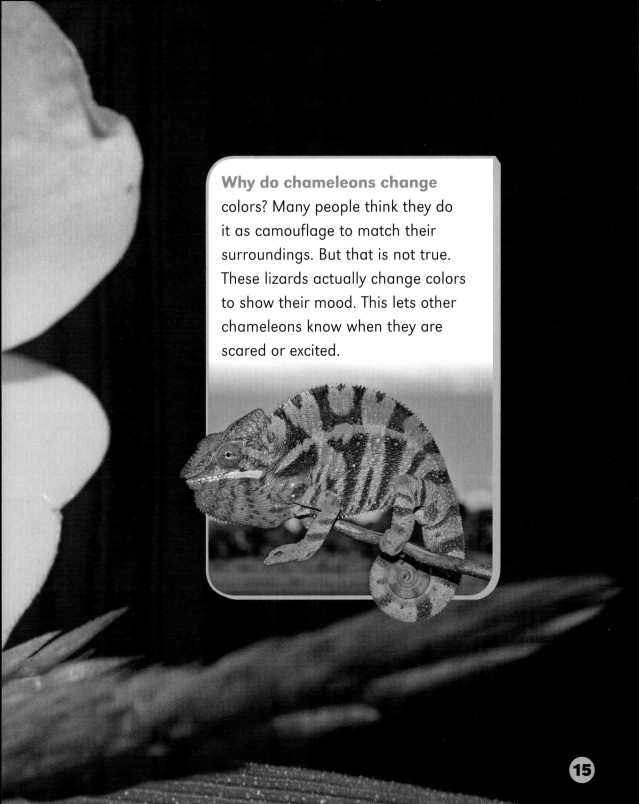

Chapter 2

Masters of Disguise

Animal disguise is another type of camouflage. Some animals pretend to be something else in their environment. The leafy sea dragon, for example, looks just like floating seaweed. Predators may mistake it for part of the plant.

Can you see the sea dragon? Look for its yellow-and-red body.

Many underwater animals use their shape to hide. This tiny sea horse is about the size of your fingernail. It looks just like coral.

Sometimes, animals **mimic**, or copy, a more dangerous animal. The black-and-yellow hoverfly looks like a wasp. But the hoverfly is harmless and doesn't sting. It pretends to be a wasp so that predators leave it alone.

Life can be dangerous for small insects. So they have developed some of the most spectacular camouflage on Earth. Some disguise themselves as parts of plants. The walking stick looks like a twig on a tree. Leaf insects are shaped like leaves. Both walking sticks and leaf insects can even sway in the breeze just like real branches and leaves.

The walking stick is the world's longest insect.

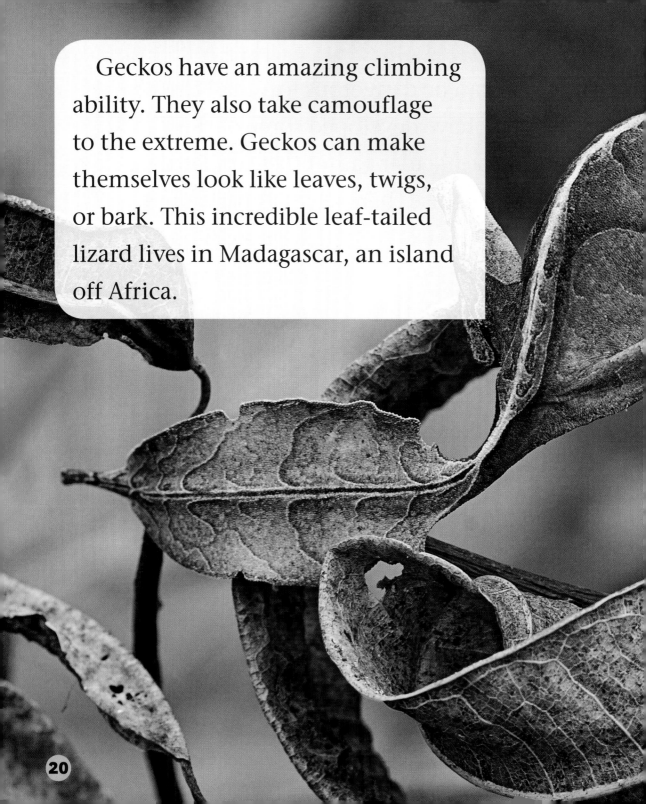

Geckos have an amazing climbing ability. They also take camouflage to the extreme. Geckos can make themselves look like leaves, twigs, or bark. This incredible leaf-tailed lizard lives in Madagascar, an island off Africa.

Ewww! Is that what it looks like? Not exactly. Some caterpillars can curl up like a pile of poo! Birds will pass on that snack.

Chapter 3

Spot the Pattern!

Now you see me, now you don't! For some animals, patterns in their fur or skin act as camouflage. A leopard's spots help it hide unnoticed in trees. This big cat scans the plains for prey. Then it leaps down and attacks with deadly force.

The tiger is another patterned big cat. Its stripes help it hide in tall jungle grasses. The stripes blur the tiger's outline against the background. This camouflage lets the cat creep up and catch prey.

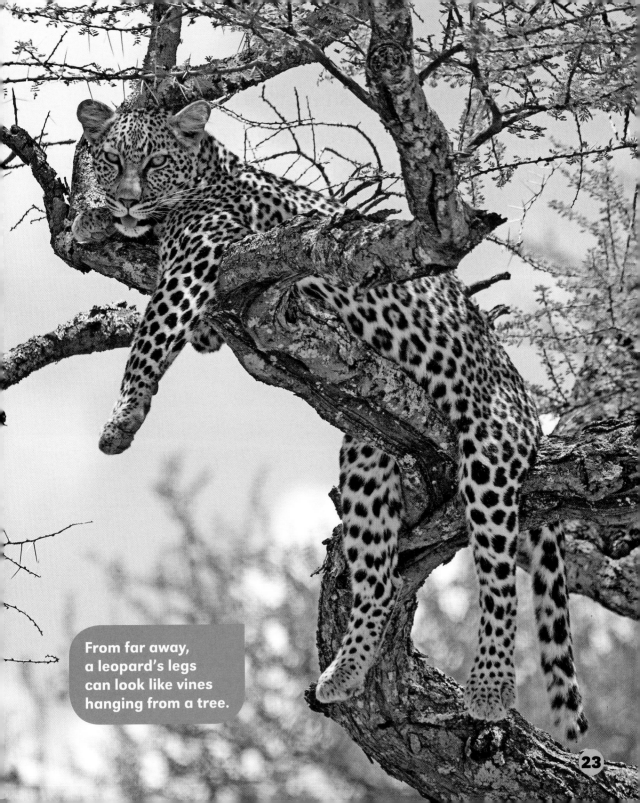

From far away, a leopard's legs can look like vines hanging from a tree.

The great white shark is not *all* white. This fearsome hunter is dark on the top and light on the bottom. It is hard for prey below to make out the shark's white belly against sunlight. From above, the shark's dark skin blends in with the water.

A great white shark is a stealthy hunter.

A giraffe's spotted fur is gold and brown. The pattern blends in with the sunlight and shadows on the African plains. Lions—giraffes' main predators—can have trouble spotting the long-necked animals as they nibble on leaves.

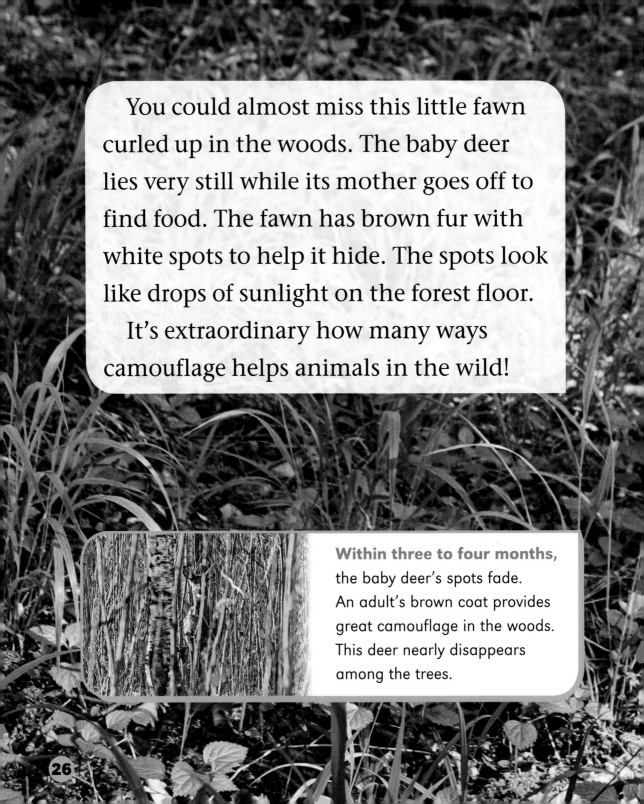

You could almost miss this little fawn curled up in the woods. The baby deer lies very still while its mother goes off to find food. The fawn has brown fur with white spots to help it hide. The spots look like drops of sunlight on the forest floor.

It's extraordinary how many ways camouflage helps animals in the wild!

Within three to four months, the baby deer's spots fade. An adult's brown coat provides great camouflage in the woods. This deer nearly disappears among the trees.